ABOUT

Jen Parker is a book publi~~ ~~...~~ing~~
authors to self-publish beau~~ ~~...with her editing,
design and publishing serv~~ices~~. She founded Fuzzy
Flamingo in September 2017. Having worked in the
publishing industry for over a decade, she's discovered
her mission is to make publishing more accessible and to
encourage more people to discover the joys of reading and
writing.

Jen started her writing career writing contributing chapters
to multi-author books, which can be found on her Amazon
author page:

https://amzn.to/3CZorqP

Writing for collaboration books gave Jen the experience
and confidence to write her first full solo book *UNFLIP:
Changing your life after a life-changing diagnosis*. The special
edition paperback can be found on her website:

https://bit.ly/Unflip_Order

MULTI-AUTHOR
SUCCESS

HOW TO PRODUCE
A WINNING
COLLABORATION BOOK

JEN PARKER

First published in 2023 by Fuzzy Flamingo
Copyright © Jen Parker 2023

Jen Parker has asserted her right to be identified as the author of this
Work in accordance with the Copyright, Designs and Patents Act 1988.

ISBN: 978-1-7391535-6-4

Editing and design by Fuzzy Flamingo
www.fuzzyflamingo.co.uk

A catalogue for this book is available from the British Library.

For my supportive Facebook community,
Fuzzy Flamingo Book Lovers.
Thanks for uplifting me and always having my back!

Contents

About the Author   i

Introduction   ix

1:   Choosing a Subject   1

2:   Getting Authors on Board   7

3:   Getting the Writing Done   11

4:   Production   15

5:   Marketing   21

Contact Me   30

Introduction

I've been in the book publishing industry, on both the traditional and self-publishing sides (and in between) for over a decade. Having worked on several types of multi-author books, I have seen first-hand how powerful they can be. I have also seen examples of things to avoid as well as routes to success. This book takes you through the basic steps needed to produce a successful collaboration book.

Why produce a multi-author book? There are lots of reasons why you might want to collaborate with fellow authors to produce a book, and here are a few examples:

1. It gives the reader the opportunity to get different viewpoints around a subject.

2. It can be the first step to becoming a published author if you've not written a book before.

3. It allows you to support each other on the way to becoming published authors.

4. It can further the reach of the book as each author will have their own (if overlapping) audiences.

Collaboration books can be very rewarding for everyone involved. It can be a gateway to becoming a published author, it can be a great marketing tool and they can make a real difference to your readers. This book is focusing on the benefits for business owners producing collaboration books, but they are not strictly limited to this type of person. I've worked on multi-author books produced by business owners in lots of different fields, including travel, health and well-being and coaching. They can be useful tools for all involved, so here are my top tips for making it the best it can be.

SECTION 1:
CHOOSING A SUBJECT

The benefits of publishing a collaboration book for your business:

1. Know, like and trust is a well-known tool for connecting with your ideal client. It is highly unlikely you have a unique business, so the best way to attract customers to buy from you over your competition is showing your personality. People buy from people, so allowing your audience to get to know you builds that personal rapport, gains their trust and shows them why they should go to you rather than other businesses in your field. Writing is a great way for your audience to get to know you and your business.

2. A new route to market. There are so many ways you can reach your ideal client: social media marketing, PR, referrals, to name just a few. Becoming a published author is an additional way for your audience to discover you.

3. Elevating your status. Becoming a published author is a huge achievement and adding this accolade to your

bio helps build your audience's trust in you. If you play your cards right and achieve a best seller, your status will skyrocket.

4. Help your readers. Teaching them something will not only show them why you're the go-to person/people in your field, it will also build those like and trust factors.

Now you know why a collaboration book can be a useful string to add to your bow, where do you begin? First things first, you need a subject matter for your book. What will it be about? This is where knowing your ideal client avatar comes in very handy.

WHO IS YOUR IDEAL CLIENT?

If you had no idea what I meant by "ideal client avatar" then that's where we need to start. Your ideal client is the one person you'd most like to buy your product or service. This doesn't mean they will be the only person who will benefit, or the only person you'd like as your client, but it is a great point on which to focus your marketing. Focusing on your niche audience makes you more likely to attract them and your client base will radiate from there. When you're looking at creating your ideal client avatar, answer questions like this:

• Are they male/female/other?

• How old are they?

- Where do they live?

- What is their likely income?

- What are their hobbies?

Once you've narrowed it down – the more specific, the better – you'll have your ideal client avatar.

This can then help you to set your marketing intention. How would you like your business – and your co-authors' businesses – to benefit from publishing a book? Remember, some of the benefits to consider are:

1. New clients finding you

2. Growing know, like, trust

3. Elevating your status

WHAT WOULD YOUR IDEAL CLIENT LIKE TO READ ABOUT?

The answers to this question will be varied and very much dependent on who they are. If your business is for new mums, perhaps they'd like to read about other mums' experiences of those early years. If you have a travel business, perhaps your ideal client wants tips on creating the perfect trip. If you are a coach, perhaps your ideal client would want to read about success stories in your field. Think about what they'd like to read and how you can fit that within your marketing intention.

You may also want to think about gaps in the market that your book could fill. Perhaps you've noticed that there are lots of books about a subject in your field, but not from a particular angle. Or perhaps you've been looking for a book to help you in your business but can't find what you're looking for, so it may be that you can bring experts together to fill that gap. This is what one of my clients Tania Taylor did with her collaboration book *The Ultimate Guided Relaxation Collection: Volume 1*: https://amzn.to/3iUDQC0 She'd found lots of relaxation script books, but as they were mostly written by just one or two people, they were a more limited resource than she wanted. She therefore filled the gap with a multi-author book of authors from different backgrounds producing an array of resources to meet the needs of varying clients for the therapists who buy the book. Think about what your client may not be able to find, put yourself in their shoes, and meet that need.

Bringing it all together

Once you know the subject you'd like for your collaboration book, the next step is to bring together authors to take part. The first step in doing so is writing a succinct, clear brief. You need to be able to convey the subject of the book in one short sentence. For example, one of the first collaboration books I worked on was by a networking group for mums in business. The authors were asked to tell their story of building their business to inspire other mums in business.

Simple. The result was that each author had a very different story to tell about what had led them to start their business and how they'd made it a success, but they all had the consistent theme of an inspirational true story that mums in business would enjoy reading.

Secondly, you need to set the parameters for your authors. Things to consider are:

1. How many authors would you like to be involved? Think about the people in your network who might like to be part of the project. If you'd like longer chapters, consider fewer authors. If you'd like shorter chapters then more authors could be included.

2. How many words would you like them to write? I would say a good aim is for a minimum total word count of 20,000 words to make a decent length book, but it can go up to 80,000 words (I'd say no more than 100,000 words, as the print cost starts getting much higher and you may well put off your ideal reader from buying it if it's too long). Most collaboration books that I work on have a word count of 3,000 words per chapter, plus 300 words for the bio for each author. If the subject matter is more complex, you may want fewer authors writing more words per chapter, or if the concept is simpler you may want more authors writing less. The thing to bear in mind with lengthier books is that, although the cover designer will be happier to have a chunkier spine to design, it could have an impact on your production

costs (more words to edit, more pages to design) and your printing costs, as the longer the book the more it costs to print. Knowing the expected word count from the beginning helps you to budget.

3. When would you like to publish? Give yourself enough time for the different stages of publishing a collaboration book: enough time for your authors to write (plus wriggle room for the inevitable stragglers, so at least four weeks), enough time for production (usually around twelve weeks for editing and design when using professionals) plus enough time for marketing and promotion ahead of the launch (at least a month works well). Work out when you need to start the project to give yourself enough time to get authors on board.

4. What do you expect from your authors? You need to be clear that they will be expected to adhere to deadlines, as well as helping with promotion when the time comes. Make it clear from the start.

5. Will you be charging your authors to take part? If so, how much? What will they get in return? This is a big factor in making the collaboration book a success, so there will be more to come later on this subject.

SECTION 2:
Getting Authors on Board

Once you have a clear brief for your authors, it's time to get them on board. Think about where you might find them. If you have specific people in mind you'd like to collaborate with, reach out to them directly. Otherwise, think about the best marketing approach for getting them on board: which social media platform do they most hang out on, are there networking groups you can utilise or would they be reading your newsletter? Use a combination and you'll have your authors on board in no time.

The importance of an author agreement

A signed author agreement gives both you and your authors peace of mind as you all know where you stand. Make it clear what your expectations are, what they can expect from you, any costs involved and what will happen to any royalties accrued (more on this later). It is a good idea to express that creative control is yours as the coordinator, you have the final say on content and design and the right to publish only what you're happy with. It saves lots of headaches down the road if your co-authors struggle to reach an agreement with the final look of the book, especially given the fact that design is subjective and there will inevitably be differences in opinion. Only accept authors into the production process once they've signed and returned the author agreement and paid anything they need to.

Should you charge your authors to be involved?

Budgeting is very important when looking at publishing a book. You should aim to at least cover your costs. The costs involved are:

1. Producing the book. This includes good editing, designing the cover (front, back and spine for a printed book, with the front used for the eBook) and the interior (known as typesetting) and publishing (including potential ISBN – more on this later – and print costs involved).

2. Marketing costs.

3. Your time (very important not to overlook this one, as publishing a book can be very time consuming).

Deciding whether to charge your authors to take part in order to cover some or all of these costs depends on a number of factors. Firstly, it depends on the authors involved. You need to consider whether your ideal authors would have the means to be able to pay to take part in the book. There are ways to keep the costs low or zero. I've had collaboration book coordinators find success with raising the production costs through various methods, including sponsorship (great for business or charity books) and crowdfunding.

If you are going to charge your authors, you'll need to consider whether you want them to cover all or part of your costs. Estimate how many hours you'd like to dedicate to the book and how much you'd charge per hour. Factor in the production (see my new dedicated collaboration book package here if you'd like to work with me: https://bit.ly/FuzzyCollabPackage) and marketing costs and divide by the number of authors you'd like as a baseline.

The collaboration book coordinators who've had success with charging higher end fees to their authors have been able to do so because of what they can offer their authors in return. Examples of this are:

1. Good marketing prospects from being a co-author and being featured by the coordinator and other authors across their platforms.

2. Coaching to create the best chapter they can. This can come in the form of writing support as well as mentoring and help to promote themselves, their business and the book. This coaching can come directly from the coordinator, as well as guest experts.

3. Being part of a community. The best collaboration books I've been part of or worked on have had a really strong sense of community. For example, a Facebook group for the authors means experts can come in and give talks, all the information for the authors can be focused in one place and the authors can get to know each other and support each other through the whole process.

Knowing what they will get in return for their investment will also help when answering the questions about why you will retain the royalties from book sales. You are putting a lot of effort into coordinating the book, you need to cover your costs, the administration involved in dividing royalties and getting them paid is a nightmare and they are getting a lot from the project.

SECTION 3:
GETTING THE WRITING DONE

You have your authors on board with a clear brief, they know how many words they're expected to write and when their first draft is expected. However, this may be the first experience of writing a chapter in a book for many, which can feel intimidating. There are a few ways you can support your authors, helping them to write the best chapter they can in a timely manner.

This is where a support group such as a Facebook group can be invaluable. You can bring in guest speakers with experience in writing to talk to your group, inspiring them to get going. Different people have different ways in which they learn best, so having a variety of guest experts coming from different perspectives helps.

For example, I've personally found success with writing a brief outline of where I want my chapter to go. For my chapter in the Mums in Business Association book *Mumpreneur on Fire 4*, I wanted to start with the early signs of joint issues in my childhood, then my diagnosis with arthritis in my gap year straight out of university, culminating with how that inspired my business as I needed a better work/life/health balance. I then use these as signposts with my first draft, which is very much a brain dump. I just write without too much thought, certainly with no editing, so that the words flow and I am able to connect to my innermost feelings, expressing them fully. This draft will include things that I would never want to share publicly, but it is cathartic to get it all out. I cut everything I don't want to share, then edit three or four times (saving as a new draft each time to refer back to if needed) to get rid of the waffle, ensure it's clear, concise, entertaining and makes sense, plus I'll check over spelling and grammar. I also send it to someone I trust to give me an honest opinion before submitting, as there will more than likely be something I've overlooked as I'm so close to it.

I know other authors with completely different methods of writing. From those with no plan at all (affectionately called "pantsers" as they're flying by the seat of their pants) right through to those who plan so much that they only have to fill in the gaps by the end of their planning! So having a range of methods discussed will help your authors forge their own path.

There are other ways you can support your authors, depending on the subject matter at hand. Tania Taylor from Tania Taylor Hypnotherapy and Psychotherapy, whose books I've had the privilege of working on, as well as having her take part in my fiction collaboration book, recorded a hypnotherapy session specifically targeted at authors. It is a brilliant starting point to get your authors in the zone, and she has generously made it free for you to download as a thank you for reading this book (it is normally £14.99) by clicking here: https://www.tania-taylor.co.uk/writers-inspiration-a-stroll-through-the-seasons/

If the subject matter of your book is very personal or highly emotive, extra emotional support may be necessary. I worked on a collaboration book for a charity supporting women affected by domestic abuse and the chapters were by women who'd experienced abuse but got through it and gone on to thrive. Not only was there emotional trauma involved with every author, there were also legal issues involved with a lot of the chapters and so emotional support from a coach plus legal support from a solicitor was needed.

Deadlines are crucial to get right. Not giving enough time may make your authors feel under too much pressure to get creative enough, or feel rushed, producing lower quality writing. Too much time and they may put it off until later and waste time. I find four weeks reaches a good balance, with all the writing coaching confined to the first week or two, leaving them at least two weeks to write and edit. Emphasising the importance of reading their stories back, why self-editing can help them produce their best work and why getting someone else to read it before they submit is very useful. This all needs to be factored in to their time management, so help them with reminders throughout their writing time with where they should be in their writing process by each point.

Above all, be empathetic. Writing and publishing a chapter can be intimidating, particularly with the more emotive subject matters. Provide support, be flexible if you need to (within reason) and remember your reasons for publishing throughout.

SECTION 4:
PRODUCTION

Once you have your authors' final drafts of their chapters, it's time to produce the book. This is something to have in place before the writing commences in order to have budgeted for it financially and in terms of timing. There are a few aspects to consider when publishing a book. My collaboration book package (https://bit.ly/FuzzyCollabPackage) has all of them covered, but if you are looking to do elements yourself or you'd like to bring in other people, here are the main points:

EDITING

I have two levels of editing: copy editing and proofreading. Both are important.

Copy editing is more in depth, looking at spelling, grammar, consistency and flow, and so is done on the Word document before typesetting. I use tracked changes so that the coordinator has the final say on accepting or rejecting the suggestions. Although the style of each chapter won't be consistent as they're written by different authors with different voices, stylistic changes such as UK or US English spelling (depending on the primary audience), overall layout of the chapters and other subjective elements should be made consistent across the board.

Proofreading is done after typesetting (designing the layout of the interior of the book how it will be printed – I use Adobe InDesign for this) on the PDF using electronic sticky notes and comments. It is only checking for remaining typos, plus any typesetting errors that may have occurred, such as line spaces in the wrong place. An editor is expected to be 80-90% accurate, so proofreading will help increase this accuracy with a second pass. Being in a different layout will also flag errors not initially seen.

Design

Typesetting is the design of the interior of the book. Before they can start, a typesetter will need to know the book size you'd like to go for, along with any branding constraints that need to be adhered to. An experienced typesetter knows the traditions of book design that other designers may not be aware of, such as page numbering starting on the first page of chapter one, with title pages having no numbering and pages of text before the first chapter (introduction, preface, etc.) numbered with roman numerals. It is important for new chapters to start on fresh pages, part pages to start on a right-hand page in printed books (not necessary in eBooks) and the typography to be consistent from the front cover, through the whole text to the back cover. If your budget doesn't stretch to a professional (although I'd highly recommend finding a way to make it work as it's so important) then make sure you do your research on how to do it and use the right software. Word is fine for eBooks, but makes typesetting for printed books much harder and won't print at as high resolution as typesetting software and so won't print as crisply.

COVER DESIGN

This can be just a front cover if you're only publishing an eBook, but needs to be the front, back and spine for a printed book. I'd recommend publishing both because they are different markets; i.e. most readers have a preference for either one or the other, not often both (I am one of the weirdos in the middle of that ven diagram!).

If you are using the collaboration book as a marketing tool for your business, it is a good idea for it to fit with your branding as well as the style of the book. Make sure you let your designer know the font choices and colours you use throughout your business, as well as sending them a high-resolution version of your logo.

When using a designer for your book cover, the outcome is usually best for both parties when you know what you'd like. A good starting point is to look at other books, especially books covering similar topics, and seeing what you like and what you don't like. This includes the ideal size of your book, so heading to physical bookshops can be helpful. Send example images of both ends of the spectrum to your designer. Have a look at image libraries (ask your designer if they have a preference – I use Adobe Stock and iStock the most because I find they have the best range for reasonable costs and good terms of use) and download samples of images that speak to you.

Your designer will need to know what text you need on the cover alongside your design ideas. What is your main title? Would you like any subtitles or taglines on the cover? Do you have any endorsements to include? Would you like your name on the cover and, if so, how would you like it to be (e.g. "edited by Jen Parker" or "a project by Jen Parker" or "a collaboration by Jen Parker")?

Most book cover designers will design the front cover first, then once the book is typeset (and they therefore know the number of pages and can work out the size needed for the spine), they will design the back cover and spine. Have a blurb (short, punchy description to encourage people to pick up and read the book) ready, along with anything else you'd like on the back cover. For example, I've worked on books that have chosen to have the authors' headshots with their names on the back.

ISBN

An ISBN is an identifier for your book that allows it to be sold by retailers. Whether you need to purchase your own ISBN depends on a number of factors, but here are the basic options:

1. If you are publishing via Amazon KDP, they give you the option of having a free ISBN. This means you allow enough space on the back cover and they will add the barcode box for you. The plus point is it's free. The downside is that other retailers tend to not like buying books with Amazon ISBNs, but if you're selling exclusively through Amazon that's not a problem. You also have less control over the look of the barcode box on the back cover.

2. If you want the option of selling to other retailers, and you'd like to publish under your own branding, you have the option to purchase your own ISBNs. In the UK, you'll need to purchase from Nielsen. If you're planning on publishing at least one further book, it is much more cost effective to purchase a block of 10, as it is less than double the price of a single ISBN. Bear in mind that you'll need to register each ISBN against each book you publish with Nielsen's Title Editor. I have a simple spreadsheet with each ISBN in one column, then I add the title, author and format (paperback, hardback, etc. – each format needs its own ISBN) each

time I assign a title so that I can't accidentally use the same ISBN twice.

3. If you are using a publishing service provider then they may offer you the option of publishing under their publishing imprint by purchasing one of their ISBNs. All of my authors now have an optional Fuzzy Flamingo ISBN included in their publishing packages, so they have the option of publishing under the Fuzzy Flamingo branding. I love seeing my little flamingo on beautiful book spines! The benefits of publishing under my branding is that I take care of all of the administration that's needed to register the book and keep it up to date. You also have the benefit of my reputation for publishing great books, plus I will be able to promote the book more across my platforms.

If you are planning to sell the eBook version of your book with multiple retailers, such as Apple, Nook and Kobo, you will need an additional ISBN for the eBook format. However, with Amazon being the biggest eBook retailer and their incentive of a much larger percentage of the royalties if you opt for their KDP Select programme for eBooks (one of the requirements is to sell the eBook exclusively through Amazon), authors often choose to publish the eBook version via Amazon KDP only and so don't require an ISBN for it. There is always the option to add an ISBN at a later date should you then want to sell on other platforms.

SECTION 5:
MARKETING

You are effectively marketing your book from the moment you start getting your authors on board. If you've done this in a public way, such as posting on social media, not only will you be piquing the interest of those who'd consider taking part as a co-author, but also of those who'd like to read the book. The key to success with book marketing is the planning, as having all your ducks in a row allows you to build on this interest, turning it into excitement at the right time.

As part of your briefing process, you should have a clear idea of when you intend to launch the book. Remember that giving yourself enough time between finishing the book production and officially launching (around four weeks allows you to get hold of printed copies and get pre-launch reviews) – but not so much time that your authors start to lose interest – is important. But the marketing process will start long before the production is finished to give maximum exposure of your book and your authors.

SLOW BURN

Once your authors are on board, you can start to slowly release details about the forthcoming book. Don't do too much early on or you'll risk alienating your potential readers as they may get fed up of hearing about it without being able to get hold of it. Authors I've worked with have found success with different methods, so you may prefer alternative tools, but I'm going to share a tried and tested launch marketing plan that authors across the board have found success with.

DURING PRODUCTION

Keeping readers updated with where the book is in terms of production is a great way to keep your audience engaged. Starting with cover design is a great visual way of presenting your book. You may even consider working on the cover design before getting the authors on board as a way to attract them, but this is a bit risky as you'll need to finance the design without knowing if your project will take off and recoup your costs. Once you have finalised the front cover, you can start by teasing it to your audience by showing part of it, asking your audience if they'd like to see more before the big reveal. When revealing the cover for the first time, there are great ways to showcase it. For example, Canva is very handy for creating social media posts (be wary of using it to create books if you're designing it yourself, as it can have issues with image rights and resolution) and the paid-for version has templates to drop in your cover design to show what it'll be like as the finished printed product.

Use elements from the cover design, such as imagery, typography and colour schemes across all of your social media marketing posts to make them eye-catching and memorable. Keep your audience up to date with key moments in production, such as "All the chapters are in and have been sent off for editing, and I can tell you you're in for a treat!" and "Here is a sneak peek of the interior design of the book and it's looking good."

Introduce your authors. Not only does this start to build the excitement for the readers by learning more about the contributors, it also gets your authors involved with the promotion at an early stage. Ask them all for a short bio and a headshot and you can introduce them in posts across your platforms over a period of time. Don't forget to tag in your authors and ask them to interact with the posts, liking, commenting on them and sharing them in order to build up the engagement and the excitement.

The run-up to launch

There are four key marketing points to cover in the run-up to launch, which work well as a four-week plan.

Week one: coming soon. Re-introduce the book by showcasing the cover and talk about what the book is about and who is involved over a few different posts.

Week two: why you're launching a collaboration book. Over a few posts, talk about who will benefit from the book, why you wanted to create it and what you're hoping the results will be.

Week three: snippets. Share key phrases and sections from different chapters. Use snippets that will showcase your book and leave your audience wanting to know more.

Week four: reviews. After typesetting is when I'd send out a PDF copy of the text watermarked with the phrase "uncorrected proof copy", which simply means it's not proofread yet and so may contain typos. Send it out to key people who are relevant to the field, for example a well-known coach may work well for a self-help book. Create posts with snippets of the reviews to show your readers why they might want to read the book.

LAUNCH DAY

My best advice for setting the date for your launch day is to give yourself enough time. Make sure you are launching on a day when you're not busy with other things, when you can devote time to not only promoting the book but interacting with people supporting your social media posts and ensuring your authors are all joining in and feeling good about the launch.

I specialise in launching on Amazon KDP, which is the print on demand platform from Amazon that works really well for collaboration books. This doesn't mean that other means of publishing and launching a collaboration book can't work well but do your research to ensure you're opting for the right path for you and your book.

I have a preference for Amazon KDP for collaboration books for a few reasons:

1. It is relatively easy to use if you know what you're doing, especially in comparison with other print on demand platforms.

2. There are no upfront costs: they don't charge you to upload or amend files, and the print costs are taken from the royalties, which lowers your financial risk. If you print a stock of books with a traditional printer, for example, you then have a minimum number you need to sell in order to recoup your costs.

3. It is easier to reach number one in your best seller categories by publishing via KDP if you do your research or use someone like me who has a good track record when it comes to best-selling authors. More on this in a moment.

There are differing opinions on the importance of ranking well in the Amazon best seller categories. Some people think that the fact you don't have to sell many copies to hit number one in some of the smaller categories makes it worthless. My opinion differs, and here are my main reasons for striving for Amazon number one best seller status:

1. Amazon won't allow you to rank in categories that aren't relevant to your book, so good research is needed to find relevant categories that aren't so competitive that you don't have a chance of ranking well. This takes time and effort, which should be celebrated.

2. You can't rank well in any category – no matter how small – if you don't make enough sales. If they are niche categories, it is generally a smaller audience for that type of book, so ranking well is relative. If you've sold well in that category, you are doing well for that niche and deserve the top spot.

3. Ranking well in the Amazon best seller categories means more people will see your book. Amazon works on algorithms much like social media, so if your book is seen to be doing well, it will be shown to more people – for example, in that section 'products related to this item' when someone views a book in similar categories to yours. Ranking well is therefore a useful marketing tool, and the longer you can rank well the better.

4. No matter what, being able to call yourself an 'Amazon best-selling author' or referring to your book as an 'Amazon number one best seller' feels and sounds great! It elevates your status, which again helps with marketing you and your book. Personally, I always

include the word "Amazon" when referring to best seller status (e.g. "I have an Amazon number one best-selling book") because there is a distinction between their lists and best seller lists from other sources, such as *The Sunday Times*.

Focusing your marketing towards launching on a particular day gives you a good shot at hitting number one in your chosen categories. The rankings are based on different factors, but the main one is selling more than the other books in your categories in twenty-four hours. Keeping sales going after this date then helps to keep you up at those top spots. This does come with planning, though. When you press publish on Amazon KDP, it can take up to seventy-two hours for them to make it live. Once you've requested your additional categories (you are allowed to choose two at the set-up stage, then up to eight in addition, but they don't let you request those additional categories until the book is live on Amazon) it can then take up to seventy-two hours for them to assign the categories. You therefore need to allow at least six days between pressing publish and officially launching, so you need some strategies around marketing the book without sending them to Amazon yet, as you don't want them to purchase before the launch date. You also need to make this clear to your authors, so that they don't accidentally encourage people to buy before you want them to.

In the run up to your launch day, it's a good idea to create graphics for your authors to share on certain days, such as the cover reveal, the snippets from the book and the reviews. Tools such as Canva are ideal for creating these with your branding and the cover design running across all of the graphics. On the day of the launch, have graphics that include the price, particularly if you are running a special offer for the launch day. This is handy because social media platforms have a tendency to limit the reach of posts that have pricing in the text because they'd rather people spend on advertising to sell products. A graphic with the price is one way of avoiding your reach being limited. It's also good to bear in mind that social media moves quickly and not everyone will see your posts about the book, so it's good to encourage your authors to post several times throughout the day. This can be with an opening post that the book is launched with the link for people to head straight to it, a live to tell your audience about the launch day (lives tend to have the best reach and engagement rates on social media) and posts to update your audience about where you are in the rankings, especially if you are climbing. I always like to drop in a post to thank people for supporting me and explaining how others can support by interacting with me throughout the day. I also have a "we made it to #1 best seller" graphic prepared for when the book gets to the top spot, as it's good to aim high!

Above all, make sure that you celebrate your launch. I've had authors organising video calls with their authors to celebrate all together, others who have met up in person to celebrate, and it always goes down well with the authors as well as their audiences. Show people how much you've put into the book and they are more likely to be interested in what you have been up to and will support you. If you have further volumes planned in a collaboration book series, it also helps prospective authors see how good it feels to be involved, thus encouraging them to sign up for the next one.

PLAN IN SOME YOU TIME

Launching a book, no matter how many you have launched, always comes with a huge spike of adrenaline. I am lucky enough to have worked on lots of books that have hit that top spot on Amazon, and I still get that adrenaline rush every time. But it is even bigger when it is your own book. My first fiction collaboration *Escape Reality* featured my short story alongside other amateur and professional authors' short stories. I soon came to realise that I needed to plan in time after the launch to wind down and to look after myself because the time and energy needed to launch a book can be a little overwhelming at times. Whether it's as simple as not booking in any meetings the day of the launch and the day after, booking yourself a massage or even going away on holiday, make sure you plan in some self-care, as it will help with the post-launch comedown and make you more likely to be willing to do it all over again! No matter how well your launch day goes, you have achieved something incredible by publishing a collaboration book, so make sure you celebrate that fact.

Contact Me

I hope you've found the information in this book useful. Reviews on Amazon help others to discover the book, so please do leave a review if you enjoyed it.

If you'd like to book a call to discuss your book project with me, you can do so via the booking form on my website. You can see what's included in the Collaboration Book Production Package here: https://bit.ly/FuzzyCollabPackage

And you can see my packages for solo authors here: https://bit.ly/FuzzyPublishingPackages

I love to connect, so join me on my socials:

Instagram:
https://www.instagram.com/fuzzyflamingodesign/

Facebook:
https://www.facebook.com/FuzzyFlamingoDesign

LinkedIn:
https://www.linkedin.com/in/jen-parker-fuzzy-flamingo/

Twitter:
https://twitter.com/FlamingoFuzzy

Printed in Great Britain
by Amazon

17763254R10025